SIX-MAN FOOTBALL

BY

J. D. ALEXANDER
ATHLETIC DIRECTOR
EAST CAROLINA TEACHERS COLLEGE
GREENVILLE, NORTH CAROLINA

EDWARDS BROTHERS, INC.
ANN ARBOR, MICHIGAN
1938

REPRINT
2010

ISBN 978-0-943736-35-8

SIX-MAN FOOTBALL

BY

J. D. ALEXANDER

ATHLETIC DIRECTOR, EAST CAROLINA TEACHERS COLLEGE
GREENVILLE, NORTH CAROLINA

EDWARDS BROTHERS, INC.
ANN ARBOR, MICHIGAN
1938

PRINTED IN U.S.A.

Lithoprinted by Edwards Brothers, Inc., Lithoprinters and Publishers
Ann Arbor, Michigan, 1938

HISTORY OF THE GAME

For several years, Stephen Epler, coaching at
Chester, Nebraska, was impressed by the fact that
hundreds of boys interested in playing football were
unable to do so due to the inability of small schools
to enroll sufficient boys to promote the game and
that the expenses incident to equipping large squads
could not be provided. In an effort to find a solu-
tion to this demand on the part of the interested
boys he set about to work out the problem by providing competition among smaller groups in a game possessing all the action, thrills, and versatility of the
regular game. Thus was evolved "Six-man" football. Thus
came into being in 1933 one of the most widely developed and most rapidly growing games of the age. The
Six-man game has all the action, thrills, and manly
attractiveness possessed by the eleven-man game.
Since smaller numbers are evolved the cost of equipping and financing a team is minimized. The growth
of the game has been phenomenal; from a small beginning in 1933 its popularity has grown by leaps and
bounds until the season of 1938 found over 1500 teams
organized and playing the game. The prospects for
its continued growth are most encouraging. Several
State High School Athletic associations are sponsor-
ing play in the game and its popularity in play-
ground and recreation centers is most encouraging.
The game is definitely with us and under proper organization and supervision will exceed even basket-
ball in popularity within a decade.

WHAT THE GAME OFFERS OF VALUE

The Six-man game gives the active adolescent
boy an opportunity to enjoy the contacts, action, and

combative urges inherent at this age level. It pro-
vides the essential fundamentals of the regular game
in a safer medium because of the smaller number involved and by the same token it is more easily fi-
nanced by the smaller schools that possess limited
financial resources with which to finance a program.
It loses none of its appeal because of the smaller
number participating. The same fundamentals are em-
ployed; the same finesse of technique; and, the same
precision of co-ordination of individual units in team
play. The Six-man game is safer because of the smaller numbers involved. The pile-up is the most frequent source of serious injuries in the eleven-man
game and this hazard is materially reduced in the
Six-man game because of the smaller numbers involved. The more open style of play minimizes injuries and encourages a better balanced game than
does the regular game. The frequent use of lateral
and forward passes encourages the development of individual skills and fundamental essentials. The
blocking, as found in the Six-man game, must of nec-
essity be better timed and more thoroughly executed
than does the blocking in the mass play formations
of the eleven-man game. The same factors apply to
tackling. Authorities admit that it is easier to
tackle a runner in mass play than in the more open
game. Fundamentals mastered in the Six-man game can
be easily transferred to the eleven-man game.

THE PLACE OF SIX-MAN FOOTBALL IN THE
PHYSICAL EDUCATION PROGRAM

The small number involved and the relative
inexpensiveness of the equipment for minimum numbers
gives Six-man football a definite place in the physical education and athletic program of the small and
medium-sized secondary schools, many of which could
not finance the eleven-man game, even if boys were
available for participation. The increased safety

and the reduction of serious and handicapping injuries encourages boys to participate who would not
attempt participation in the regular eleven-man game.
The Six-man game can be used to supplement the regular game in the larger school and permit a broader
participation than would otherwise be possible. It
offers a find opportunity for developing skill, co-
ordination and mastery of essential fundamentals necessary for successful participation in the eleven-
man game later.

The Six-man game is ideally fitted to intra-
mural play and to the tournament style of play frequently sponsored in county athletic organizations.
It has a definite place in the field of organized
recreation and on supervised playgrounds. Since it
is less dangerous and injuries are less frequent it
is adapted to sand-lot and unsupervised areas, although the importance of adequate equipment and careful supervision can not be overstressed. For the
small rural school of secondary rank the Six-man
game of football opens up new vistas of athletic opportunity.

THE ORGANIZATION OF THE GAME

For the game to succeed as an interschool
competitive sport adequate organization and proper
supervision must be provided. Such an organization
should be composed of schools within a limited area
to minimize travel and loss of time involved in such
travel. Experience has found that leagues comprising
four or more teams are best adapted to successfully
carrying out interschool competition. The eight-
team league with all the member schools located within a radius of thirty miles can be organized within
most counties in the eastern section of the United
States whereas a larger area would be necessary in
the western section or in the more sparsely settled
areas.

The organization should comprise schools
having similar strength as regards material, enroll-
ment, and financial resources. A fairly well-balanced
program of competition should be arranged if the
program of competition in Six-man football is to be
most satisfactory to all concerned. Certain rules
regarding eligibility, competition, rules interpretation, and officiating must be a part of the central
organization of the league and some one must assume
the responsibility for carrying out and enforcing
such eligibility and league rules and regulations.
The county athletic organization is admirably fitted
for administering such a program. Capable officials
must be provided and it may be necessary to hold
rules interpretation meetings and clinics for the
training of Six-man officials if the game is to
reach the maximum of its potentialities.

Existing organizations can carry on the work
with a minimum of effort. Some central organization
must assume the responsibility of carrying out the
organization and administering of interschool competition if the greatest good is to accrue from
participation in the Six-man game. Such organizations can aid the schools materially by pooling
resources in purchasing equipment; providing officials; setting up standards of eligibility; arranging educational meetings for coaches and administra-
tors; and, arranging helpful publicity.

COACHING SIX-MAN FOOTBALL

The duties of training the team will involve
several vitally important duties if the game is to
succeed in the Physical Education and Athletic program of our modern schools. The duties of the coach
may well be divided into four major divisions:
(1) duties pertaining to the organization, purchase,
and maintenance of equipment and supplies; (2) duties
having to do with conditioning the boys and providing

those skills which will minimize injuries and provide the greatest degree of safety in participation;
(3) teaching fundamentals and skills; and, (4) developing team play with all the factors that contribute
to team oneness.

The selection of equipment and the maintenance of equipment after its purchase is one problem
that should require a careful study of the finances,
needs, and facilities available. All equipment should
be purchased by competitive bid with every detail of
quality and safety carefully evaluated. The most important item of equipment is the shoes. Ill-fitting,
poorly-constructed shoes result in blisters, abra-
sions, and painful callouses that will impair the efficiency of the player. Shoulder pads should provide
a maximum of safety with as much freedom as possible.
Two-piece pants are preferred as one set of good,
well-constructed pads will outlast several pairs of
skeleton pants or shells. The kidney pads should be
well made of durable materials and padded for the
greatest protection. The pads should be as light as
is consistent with safety. Safety should not be
sacrificed for lightness. For schools with limited
budgets duck pants are best for the money. The helmets should give adequate protection and every par-
ticipant in football should be required to wear a
helmet. Blocking pads should be provided for those
boys that handle the blocking assignments in the
backfield. Adequate protective equipment should be
provided, although one cannot estimate protective
values by the price tag. Equipment approved by the
National Federation of High School Athletic Associations has been tested for safety and value and the
approval of this organization as designated by its
approval tag usually connotes a good value. Adequate
first-aid supplies and equipment should be provided
and all injuries given prompt first-aid treatment.

CONDITIONING

Systematic conditioning and well-directed
training technics will reduce the number and sever-
ity of injuries. The conditioning should be gradual
and should be begun only after each boy has had a
thorough physical examination and pronounced as fitted for participation by a reputable physician, preferably his family physician. The training period
should be organized so that the various fundamentals
can be taught as the boys develop their bodies. A
thorough knowledge of the various fundamentals is a
great factor in reducing injuries. Healthful living
habits and practices should be taught as a definite
part of the conditioning and training schedule. De-
velopmental exercise planned to bring about a well-
balanced all-around development should be a part of
the conditioning program. The work should not be too
rigorous nor strenuous or damage may result. The author believes that many boys have their health impaired by too strenuous activities during the period
of adolescence. As strength is developed the work
can be graduated accordingly. Regular hours should
be encouraged and the importance of sleep stressed.
The average high school boy does not realize the
vital part sleep plays in building vigor and health.
The average high school boys needs eight hours of
sleep at regular hours if he is to reach the peak of
physical efficiency and athletic ability.

TEACHING FUNDAMENTALS

In teaching the basic fundamental skills several approaches are used; demonstrations by the coach
and other skilled performers; verbal explanations;
motion pictures, preferably with parts in slow motion,
of outstanding performers in action; and, by the use
of game situations. Each type of approach has

certain advantages but the demonstration method
will predominate because of the limitations adherent
to the application of the other types of instruction.
In presenting a fundamental by means of the demonstration it is important that the demonstrator make
clear the various stages or steps in the movement
or activity. For example, the charge of the lineman
might be analyzed into its essential parts; as,
stance, footwork, direction of movement, application
of power, desirable areas of contact; and, arm co-ordination. When the prospective player has grasped
the significance of the various steps and the order
of their sequence he has done much toward making
them applicable to game conditions. As the various
elements in the sequence are mastered such essential
elements as balance, rhythm, and timing are brought
out and co-ordinated into the general phases of the
completed fundamental. This arrangement of sequence
is vitally important if the student is to be made to
realize the most from his efforts. Successful teaching of fundamental skills and their use under game
conditions determines the success of the coach.

MOLDING THE TEAM

        Once the coach has taught the various indi-
viduals the basic fundamentals of the game his most
difficult assignment is begun. He must now co-ordi-
nate the six individuals into a team. This necessi-
tates an organization of the varying abilities into
a machine-like unit capable of executing their varying skills against an ever-changing opposing unit
under a variety of uncontrolled conditions. To do
this skillfully the coach must know the individual
strengths, abilities, and weaknesses of each of the
boys on the team. He must know their emotional sta-
tus; their ability to react to varying situations in
divergent settings. The better he knows all the factors that can influence the conduct patterns of his

players the better he can blend the various units
into a team. The coach must be a student of adolescent psychology in its practical phases. He must
command the respect of his charges and at the same
time be their master. He must be able to teach them
the things that will be of most worth to them and to
the team. Many times this teaching goes on against
the definite wishes of the player. He is convinced
against his own wishes in many cases. The coach
must be able to demonstrate the value of the suggestions if they are to be accepted. The coach must be
fair in all his dealings with the boys if his work
is to net the greatest returns. Once the boys lose
confidence in him his efficiency is marred and team
play will wane. The coach can contribute much to
team success by his confidence and enthusiasm.

CHARGING

     The initial charge of a football player plays
an important part in the effectiveness of his play.
The fast-charging, hard-hitting, alert line seldom
leaves the field with the sting of defeat. The fast-
charging back will lose little ground on any play.
The charge is all the more important in Six-man football because of the limited number in the line of
scrimmage and the openness of the play. A slow charging lineman cannot stop the defense and loss after
loss will result. Every lineman in Six-man football
must develop a fast, sustained charge of almost ex-
plosive force if he hopes to be of most worth to his
team. His stance, preliminary to the charge, must be
comfortable, strong, and capable of providing maximum
speed and power. The stance of the center varies.
The center assumes a stance with the feet wide apart;
the toe of the left foot being on a line with the
heel of the right foot; the knees are bent; the back
straight and the head up. He should be comfortable
and in position to direct his charge in any direction.

His stance must withstand a defensive charge direct-
ed at him from the front or either side. His initial move must be a powerful thrust of the body in
the direction of the charge. The charge is main-
tained by a series of driving, digging, chopped steps
with the feet parallel and perpendicular to the line
of scrimmage.

PASSING

        Passing plays a most important part in Six-
man football and offers the coach and players unlim-
ited potentialities in developing a diversified attack. Both lateral and forward passing can be developed advantageously. At least one pass must be a
part of every offensive play, if Epler's official
rules are followed. Rule VI, states, "The offensive
ball carrier, receiving the ball from the center,
must pass the ball to a teammate before he crosses
the line of scrimmage." This emphasis upon the passing game tends to make the game safer, more interest-
ing to both spectators and players, and, encourages
a diversified attack.
        Two types of lateral passes are widely used;
(1) the lob or floating pass; (2) the spiral or bul-
let type. The first is used on short laterals or
under conditions which make ball handling difficult.
Much time should be spent in its mastery. The spiral
is used where distance and accuracy are required and
requires more experience and better timing than does
the lob pass. Most coaches spend from twenty to
thirty percent of their practice periods in perfect-
ing their passing attack and feel the time is well
spent. In practice the work should be done under
conditions similar to game conditions and the receivers should be forced to break away from opponents in
situations similar to those found to exist in a game.
        In planning the passing attack much atten-
tion must be given to the development of the forward

passing phase of Six-man football. Since a forward
pass may be made from any point behind the line of
scrimmage the ball carrier can turn most any play
into a forward pass if he can find an eligible re-
ceiver open for his throws. He must be alert to any
opportunity to take advantage of any weakness of the
defense that makes a forward pass possible from a
running play of any type should an opportunity present itself.

      Every forward pass should start as a running
play in order to deceive the defense or should have
its initial movements similar to a running play in
the teams repertoire of plays. If a team has an outside end play that is successful as a ground gainer
a forward pass thrown from a similar beginning to the
end on the opposite side should and materially to the
strength of the running plays as the game progressed
and need for variety comes.

      A passing attack will fail if it has no run-
ning attack and vice versa. A good forward passing
attack strengthens the whole offensive set-up and
makes a good passing attack more successful.   The
passer must learn to hide his intention to pass and
to maintain this deception until he raises his arm
for the toss of the ball. He must follow the receiv-
er without telegraphing his intentions. A good
peripheral vision, either natural or acquired, is
a valuable asset to the deception of the passer. A
quick snap movement that can begin with the throwing
arm and the ball in a natural ball-carrying position
adds to the effectiveness of the passing attack. In
training the passer defensive linemen should rush
him in his practice sessions to enable him to throw
accurately under game conditions. He should practice
getting off his passing with his opponents literally
swarming over him. Some of this ability may come
naturally but hard consistent practice forms the
basis of a successful passing attack.

      Have the receivers practice catching passes
while closely guarded and going at full speed

straight down the field and at varying angles from
the line of scrimmage. Much practice must be had
working under adverse weather conditions in order to
master the handling of the pass under poor conditions.
A wet muddy ball requires more careful timing than
does a pass made under ideal conditions. The wind
can influence the timing and speed of a pass and
cause fumbles unless the individual has mastered
these influences by constant practice. Forward pass
receivers should master the lateral so that they can
pass the ball back to a team mate in a more favored
position for a gain if and when they are about to be
tackled. An attack built around a combination for-
ward-lateral passing offense is hard to stop, especially if the offense has a decent running attack to
provide variety and deception. The passer and re-
ceiver must work together for prolonged periods if
their work is to be of most value. Inaccurate passing is dangerous. Confidence can best be established
by having the boys work together until they have mastered such elements as, accuracy, timing, and deception,

KICKING

        In Six-man football kicking is both an of-
fensive and a defensive fundamental. All phases of
the kicking art should be mastered and used. Punting is the background around which the team attack
should be built. Punters should master placement
and distance kicking, as well as the ability to get
kicks off rapidly under the stress of competition.
The well-placed quickly kicked punt is a fine defensive weapon and plays an important part in the offensive strategy of the team. A part of every practice
period should be devoted to kicking practice and to
defensive play against the kick.
        The quick kick is one of the finest offen-
sive threats in Six-man football. The open formations

and the small numbers of players involved make it
difficult to get off accurate quick kicks, but once
they are mastered are one of the finest offensive
weapons at the disposal of the offensive field general.
        The place kick plays an invaluable part in
the Six-man game. It is used on the kick-off and in
an attempt for field goals. A conscientious effort
must be made to perfect this phase of the game. The
loss of many games can be traced to ineffective kicking for extra points or the failure to kick a field
goal at a critical time. The coach must convince
his boys of the value and effectiveness of this important phase of the game. It adds to the teams
confidence and to its effectiveness.

                    OFFENSIVE PLAY

        The style of offensive play used in planning
the season will depend upon the ability, experience,
and quantity of material available, and to a certain
degree, upon the types of defense used by the various
opposing teams played during the season. A series of
several plays should be built around each of two or
three offensive formations. The short formation has
been found very useful in planning an attack based
upon deception, kicking, and passing. It lacks certain essentials necessary for an attack based pri-
marily upon power but with boys of average ability
and experience can be made the basis of a splendid
running attack. With clever ball handling and an
alert passer and kicker, it will prove an invaluable
offensive attack. It pleases the spectators and is
liked by the players because of its versatility.
        The ends, in the short punt formation, play
from three to five yards on either side of the snapperback. The quarterback plays one to one and one-
half yards back of the line of scrimmage and slightly
to one side of the center. The halfback plays directly

back of the quarterback, a distance of one to two
yards, depending on his speed and the defensive set-
up. The fullback plays from five to seven yards directly back of the center. The quarterback must b
a good ball handler and a willing hard blocker. Success of the offensive attack depends much upon his
ability to handle the ball and to charge out any defensive men who break by men assigned to charge them
out.

The halfback plays an important rôle in the
success of the Six-man football offense. He must be
a clever broken field runner; a good pass catcher;
and, a hard, sure blocker. He carries the ball on
many of the end-runs and reverse plays and is the
logical man to be open for short forward passes over
the center and in the flat zones. On mouse-trap
plays he takes the defensive man as he comes through
and his success in blocking will decide the effectiveness of the reverses and mouse-trap plays.

The fullback, or tailback, must be able to kick
and pass and should have some ability as a ball carrier. He can make himself invaluable by his effective punting and passing. A good quick kicker in the
tailback position can add much to the effectiveness
of the running attack, because of his keeping the defense spread with the safety man well back from the
line of scrimmage. An accurate passer playing the
halfback position can add further to the effectiveness of the offensive attack by presenting a varied
attack and constant threat from the various fundamental phases of the attack. In planning the offense,
each series of plays from a given formation should
have passes, reverses, line smashes, and spinners
starting in the same way so as to add to the offensive deception and thus strengthen the attack. The
short punt formation is especially adapted to this
varied form of attack and presents a versatile weapon
in the hands of the quarterback. The open attack is
the basis of Six-man football and the short punt formation offers great possibilities in this style of
attack. Several plays from short punt formation follow.

Short Punt Formation

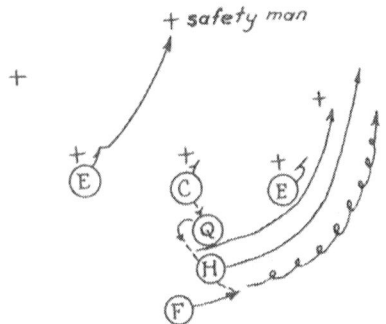

End Run to Strong Side Ball. Is
snapped to Q, who spins and laterals to F. H runs interference
for F.

Effective against a slow charging
defensive end.

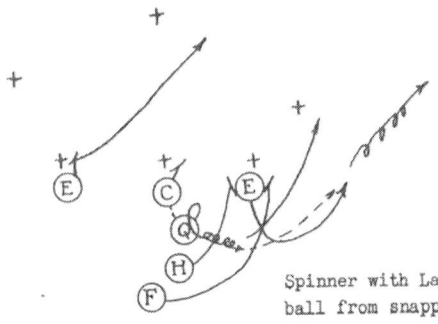

Spinner with Lateral to End. Q takes
ball from snapperback, spins and starts
as if for an end run. H and F go for
the defensive end. The strong side offensive end pulls out and goes wide to
outside to receive lateral from Q as Q
approaches line of scrimmage. After
making the lateral Q goes for secondary.

Short Punt Formation

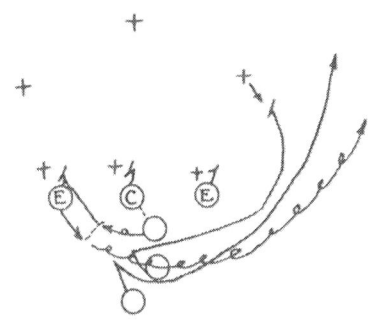

Fake End Run with Reverse to
Strong Side. Q takes the
ball and starts to the weak
side.   He laterals to E who
pulls out and drives hard
for the strong side. H and
F fake a start for the weak
side; reverse and lead the
interference for E as he
goes off strong side.

Effective against linemen
that drift in the direction
of the ball and are not
alert. Offensive linemen
block to keep men from coming in behind and overtak-
ing E.

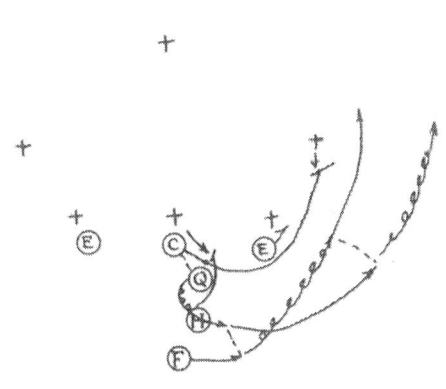

Double Lateral with
Mouse Trapping. The
ball is snapped to
Q who fades back and
makes a short later-
al to F. Q cut be-
hind F and takes a
lateral from F as F
approaches a would
be tackler. C pulls
out and runs inter-
ference for F and Q.
H mouse traps the
defensive center as
he pulls through to
tackle Q or F. An
effective block by H
will make this play
work if E can handle
his man.

Short Punt Formation

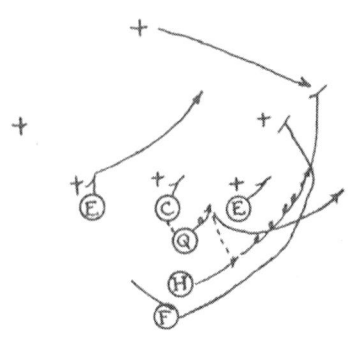

Double Lateral with End Run to
Strong Side of the Line. Q
takes the ball from the snapperback, fades in almost to
line of scrimmage and laterals
to H. H drives hard off defensive end and when about to
be tackled makes a lateral
pass to Q who has cut behind
him to the outside.

Good against a team that is
expecting a pass.

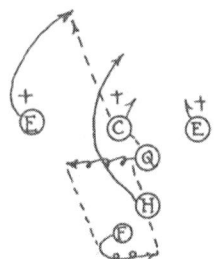

Forward Pass from Short Punt
Formation. The ball is
snapped to Q who drives to
weak side as for an end run, F
hesitates momentarily and
takes a lateral from Q and
runs to right and makes an
optional forward pass to either E, H, or Q. Effective
following a reverse play or
a series of line plays. F
must be a fast accurate passer.

Short Punt Formation

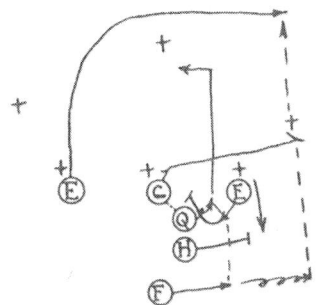

Forward Pass Following
Reverse Play to Strong
Side End. Q takes the
ball, goes to his right
and hands the ball to
the end who in turn lat-
erals it to F who passes
to the weak side end who
has crossed over behind
the defensive line of
scrimmage. Effective
against charging secon-
dary men.

* * * * * *

Tandem Pass

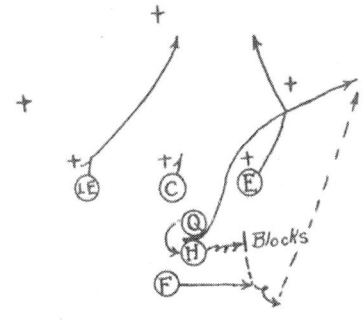

Tandem Pass. Q takes
the ball from center and
spins; passing the ball
to H as he completes his
spin. H laterals the
ball to F and protects
until E or Q gets open
for forward pass. F
passes to either Q or E.
L draws the safety man
away from the play.

Unbalanced Formation

The unbalanced formation offers several advantages in Six-man football offered by no other formation in that more power can be thrown
against the defense on sweeps around end or on line smashes. The
left end snaps the ball and at the same time is eligible under the
rules for forward passes and to carry the ball on end around plays.
This enables the coach to vary his attack and to use all his men in
ground gaining capacities.

This formation is good for smashing through the line when the offense
has a powerful line plunger in the F position. H should be a good
blocker and fine interferer. A small boy that can handle the ball
well and who possesses football sense can qualify for the Q position.
The author has known one team of championship caliber to play a nine-
ty-pound boy in this position with marked success and without a handicapping injury all season.

The left end lines up as snapperback. The center plays from three to
four yards to his right; the right end plays three to three and one-
half yards to the right of the center as diagrammed. Q and H play in
the hole between the snapperback and the center and two yards back of
the line of scrimmage. "F" plays four to five yards back of the snapperback. Several plays from this formation are diagrammed.

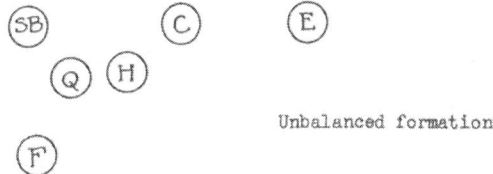

Unbalanced formation

Unbalanced Formation

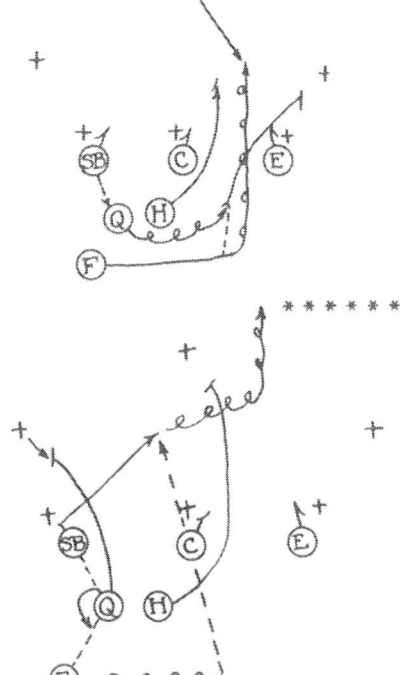

Effective for Deception and
Passes. Line smash from
fake end-run. Q takes the
ball from the snapperback
and starts to the right as
if for an end-run; laterals
to F and drives for secondary, leading the interference
for F who cuts back for a
smash inside his end.

* * * * * *

Forward Pass to Snapperback.
Q takes the ball from the
snapperback and spins, lat-
eralling the ball to F as
he spins. F cuts back and
makes a forward pass to the
snapperback SB. Others
handle assignments as diagrammed.

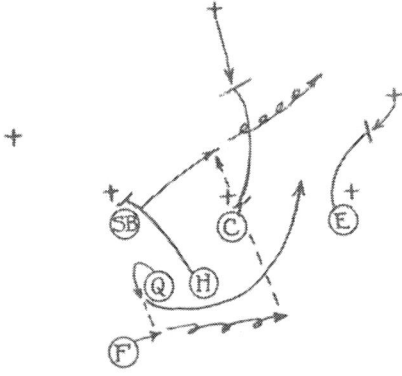

* * * * * *

Forward Pass to Snapperback.
This pass has the advantage
of having an effective cross
block used on the defensive
end, as he plays in front of
the snapperback. The snapperback cuts behind H as H
blocks his man and tries to
get open for a short pass
over the center. Q laterals
the ball to F and protects
until F gets his pass off and
rushes up field alert for a
lateral from SB.

Unbalanced Formation

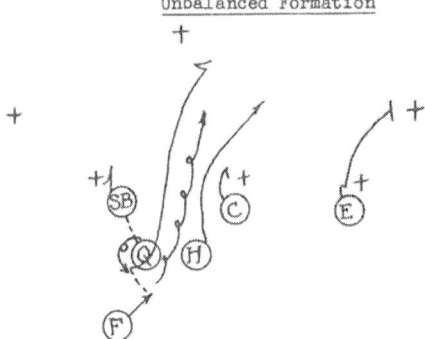

Line Smash from Unbalanced Formation. Q takes the ball from SB on
snapback, spins and laterals to F. Q leads the interference for F. SB
drives his man out; C charges his man out with a powerful charge; H
goes for secondary. With fast backs this play is very good following
a series of forward pass plays from the same formation.

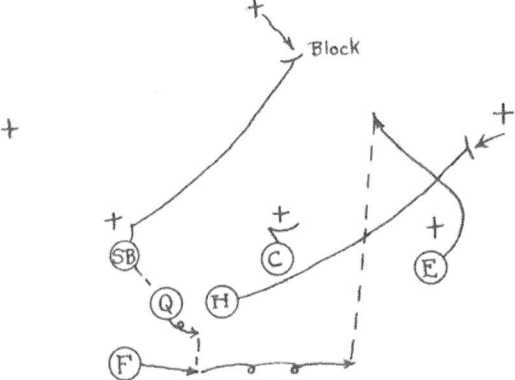

Quick Forward Pass Play. Q takes ball from snapperback and quickly
laterals to F. F drives to his right and makes a quick pass to E who
has cut back toward the center in front of the safety man.

Triangular Formation

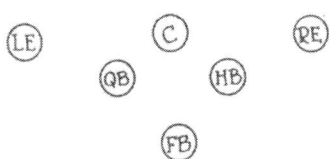

The Triangular Formation is strong against teams playing a spread defense and against teams that are expecting a superior passing attack as it is versatile enough to offer a very varied attack under all conditions against a spread defense.

The ends play two to three yards out from the center with the QB and the Hb splitting the distances between the center and the ends and one to one and one-half yards back of the line of scrimmage. The fullback (FB in the diagram plays four to five yards directly behind the center).

The best defense is a three-two-one man-for-man defense with the linemen playing their man straight on and charging hard to the point of the triangle.

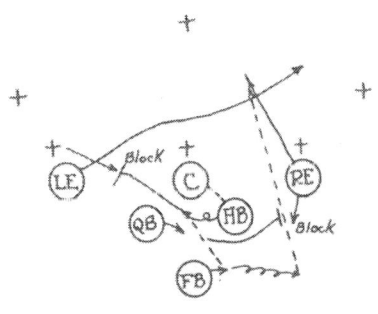

Forward Pass, Triangular Formation. HB takes the ball from C on the snapback and starts to his left; fakes a lateral to QB and laterals to FB. QB protects as FB passes to RE directly over center. LE crisscrosses in front of RE to decoy defense out of position. HB blocks defensive end after lateral passing to FB.

Triangular Formation

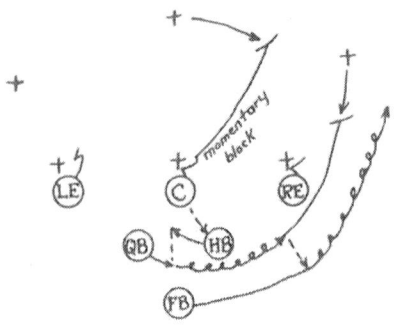

Double Lateral with Reverse
End Run. HB takes the
snapback and starts to his
left; laterals to QB who
runs parallel to line of
scrimmage until past end
and then laterals to FB
and leads off defensive
end. C blocks his man
momentarily and then
drives for the secondary.

This play is very effec-
tive following a forward
pass from a reverse or
against a slow defense.

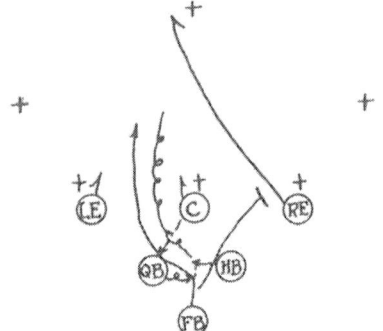

Reverse Play from Triangular Formation. The ball
is passed to the QB, he
fakes handing the ball to
FB and then laterals it
behind FB to HB who runs
off the center with FB
leading the interference.
Effective against a loaf-
ing or slow center following a series of forward
passes.

Triangular Formation

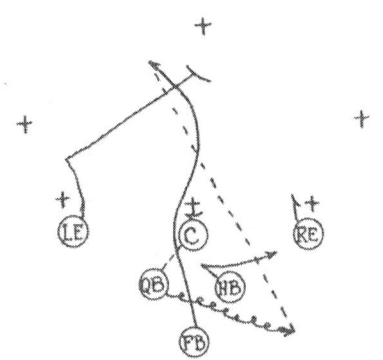

Forward Pass Play from
Triangular Formation.
QB takes the snap from
center fakes to FB and
then to HB and cuts
back with HB protect-
ing and passes to FB.
Should FB be too close-
ly covered the pass can
go to LE. Good follow-
ing the reverse play
above.

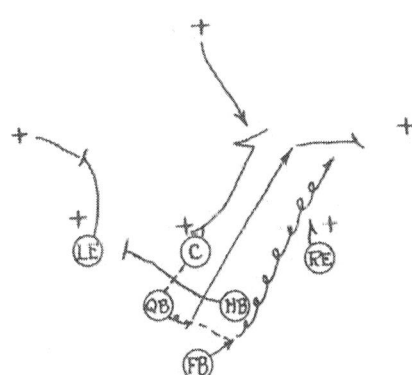

Line Smash from Trian-
gular Formation. QB
takes the ball from
center and fakes a
short shovel pass to
HB and passes the ball
to FB and leads him
through the line.

LE goes for the defen-
sive back.

HB blocks the defen-
sive end.

Triangular Formation

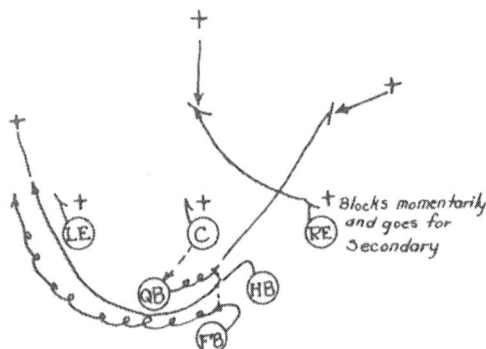

End Run Play, Triangular Formation. QB takes the snapperback and fakes a lateral pass to HB. QB lobs the ball to FB and goes hard for the secondary. HB leads the interference for FB. Effective against a slow charging defensive end.

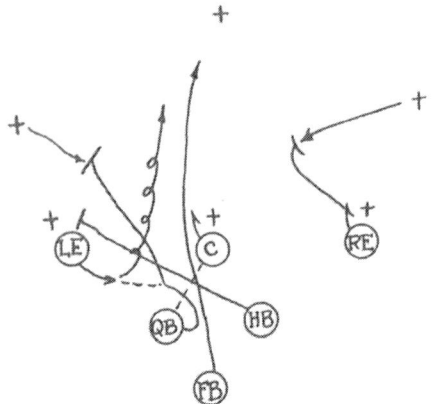

Fake End Around Play with Smash through Line. QB takes the ball from the center and hesitates for two counts. HB is in motion when the ball snaps and cuts through to block the defensive end. FB leads the interference. QB hands ball to LE and leads him for smash through the line.

Triangular Formation

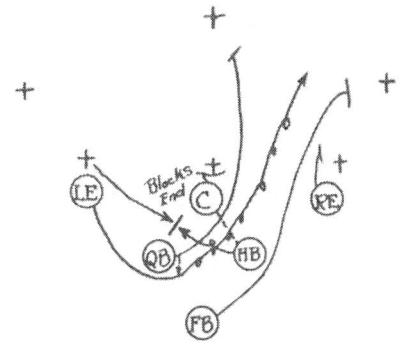

Lateral with Reverse End Around. HB takes the ball from center and drives hard to left; passes ball to left end, LE, who cuts around center with QB and FB leading interference. Very effective if properly timed. Especially good against a smashing defensive right end. Difficult to time correctly.

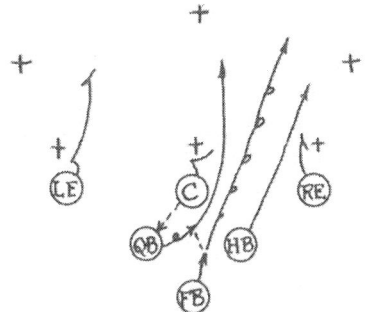

Triangular Formation for Line Smash. QB takes the snapback from C and fakes a smash and laterals to FB and leads interference for FB through line. Requires a hustling QB who can pass accurately at full speed.

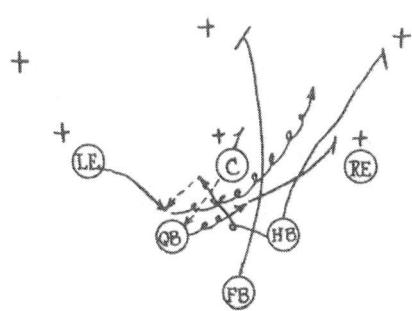

Double Reverse Through Line. QB takes the snapback from C and goes hard to the right. QB passes to RE as RE cuts close to center and passes back to LE as he cuts behind him. LE cuts to the right for a line plunge behind the interference of HB and FB.

REGULATION SIX-MAN FOOTBALL PLAYING FIELD

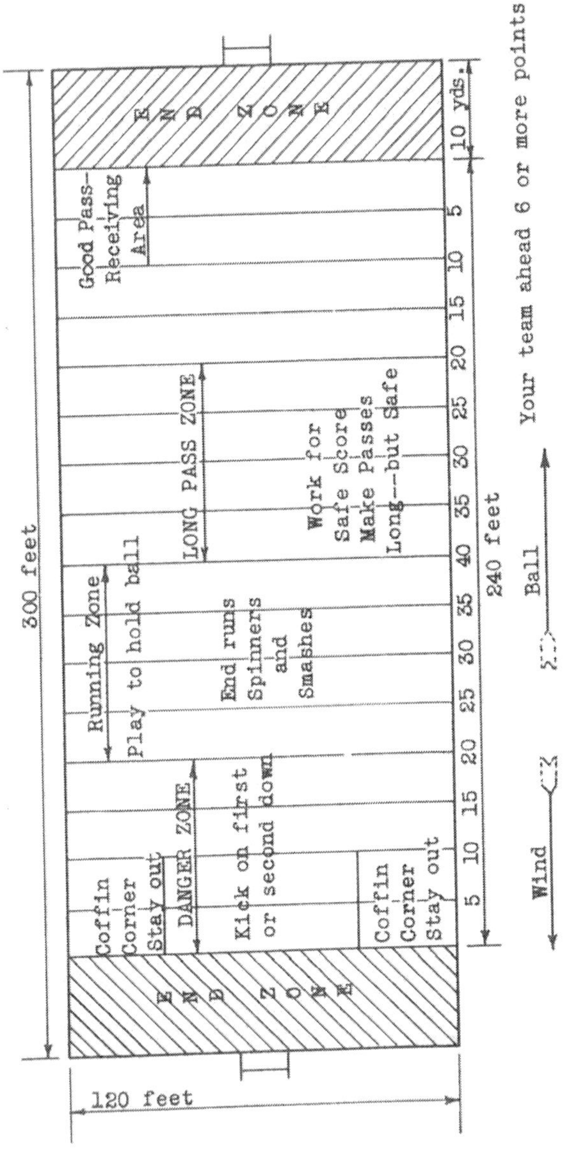

300 feet
120 feet
240 feet
10 yds.
END ZONE
END ZONE
Good Pass-Receiving Area
LONG PASS ZONE
Work for Safe Score
Make Passes Long--but Safe
Running Zone
Play to hold ball
End runs Spinners and Smashes
DANGER ZONE
Kick on first or second down
Coffin Corner Stay out
Coffin Corner Stay out
5 10 15 20 25 30 35 40 35 30 25 20 15 10 5
Your team ahead 6 or more points
Ball
Wind

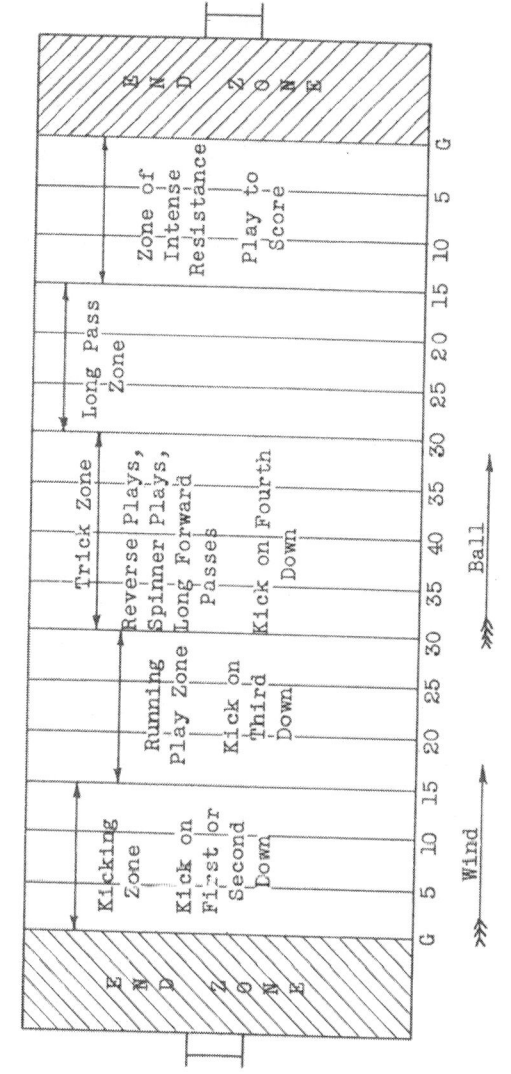

OFFENSIVE STRATEGY MAP. SCORE EVEN OR NO SCORE

DEFENSIVE PLAY

An effective defense must be built upon a thorough knowledge of the fundamentals of hard fast charging, strong sure tackling, effective use of the body and hands, and a knowledge of game conditions. No team will be badly defeated that can execute all these fundamentals thoroughly. Much time must be spent on developing a hard defensive charge and methods of effective use of the hands to ward off blockers. Dummy scrimmage and blocking practice against a well-stuffed dummy will do much to build the confidence and skill necessary for successfully executing a superior type of charging. The defense must be alert to sense new situations brought about by failure of team mates to handle their assignments and this type of experience can be secured only through well-directed scrimmage, using both dummies and men to perfect timing and co-ordination.

A defensive attitude should be developed and the boys should be taught to realize that a score prevented is a score made. An aggressive defense well coached in the execution of the various defensive fundamentals will never suffer wide marginal defeats. After fundamentals are mastered in dummy scrimmage and against tackling dummies the boys should be encouraged to apply their skill against men in action under game conditions to master the timing and co-ordinations necessary for successful execution under game conditions.

Good defensive work should be recognized and the boys given credit for the superiority of their performances. Every effort should be made to inspire confidence and to build enthusiasm for defensive work.

Every man should be taught the various blocks and the conditions under which they are most effective. Every effort should be made to have him practice blocking daily under conditions most near

actual game conditions. The rolling block and other
open field blocks should be stressed and their cor-
rect execution demanded. No player should be ex-
cused from blocking and tackling practice for these
two basic fundamentals are the keystones of the defense.

In skull practices and in discussion meetings the coach should emphasize what is to be ex-
pected under varying conditions and at various loca-
tions on the field and in different strategical situations. Alertness must be encouraged at all times
and the boys must be impressed with the fact that
anything can happen on the defense. Encourage think-
ing. and talking while on defense. Every man must be
alert for evidences of the unexpected and must communicate his findings to his team mates.

DEFENSIVE FORMATIONS

        No one defensive formation will adequately
meet all offensive situations at all times. For
most situations a team of high school boys of average ability can best use a three-two-one defense.
The three men on the line must be alert to line
plays and must maneuver their men to get through to
the secondary if they are most effective in breaking
up plays. The secondary defensive men must be alert
for passes, reverse plays, and for smashes that have
penetrated their line. They should play one to two
yards outside and from three to seven yards behind
the defensive ends; their position varying with the
strategical situation, the personnel of the opposing
team, wind conditions, and time left to play.   On
fourth down with small yardage required they should
probably pull in to fill the holes between the defensive center and the end, especially near the goal
line. On punts the men in the secondary must block
ends coming down field and must interfere for the
safety man when once he has the ball.

The tertiary or safety man will play directly opposite the center of the power of the opposing
team and from twelve to twenty yards from the line
of scrimmage. This distance depending upon the yardage to go, the down, the strategical situation, and
the location on the field. He must be a sure tackler,
fast deceptive runner, and a sure pass or punt
catcher. He must sense plays and possess that rare
quality we frequently speak of as football sense. His
ability to catch and run back punts and intercept
passes will determine his value to the team in an offensive way. His position is especially strategic
since he is often the interchanging factor between offense and defense.
        The safety man is the defensive field gener-
al. He is in position to see plays and foretell fu-
ture happenings and should communicate such evidences
to his team mates. He should call changes of position for his team on defense and should be alert for
opportunities to use his men to best advantage. He
should keep the strategical situation in mind at all
times and should be alert for glaring evidences of
weakness on the opposing team; and, once these weaknesses are located should use them to his team's advantage.

SUGGESTIONS FOR THE DEFENSE

        Always be alert; never permit yourself to re-
lax mentally or physically.
        Remember the best pass defense is to rush
the passer. Rush hard into the offensive backfield
area and tackle the man with the ball.
        Smash through, but be alert for laterals and
cut-back plays.
        Watch for men laying out along the sidelines
and flat zones.
        If the Offensive men let you through without
resistance be alert for mouse-trap plays or quick

passes. Always sense that something is wrong if the
offense offers little or no resistance.

Be alert for passes if there is large yardage to gain on third or fourth downs.

The center and the ends should rush the kicker at all times. Rushing the kicker is the best defense against punting. Use it.

Never permit the offense to wrestle you or
slow down your charge into their backfield.   Get
Through.

Remember the strategical situation;

a. The down

b. The yards to go

c. Time to the quarter, half, or end of game

d. The Offensive teams strongest attack

e. Their pass receivers and their best
   blockers

f. Who kicks for them

Play the ball when in their territory. Get
the man with the ball and the others can go.

Take time out if exhausted. Do not try to
bluff the offense. Talk the situation over while
resting.

Take time out after the opponents have
started rally. Ask for substitutes when injured.
Remember a strong inexperienced man is better than
a crippled star.

Play your opponents weaknesses; get the jump
on him and you can handle him. Never hesitate, but
charge fast and hard.

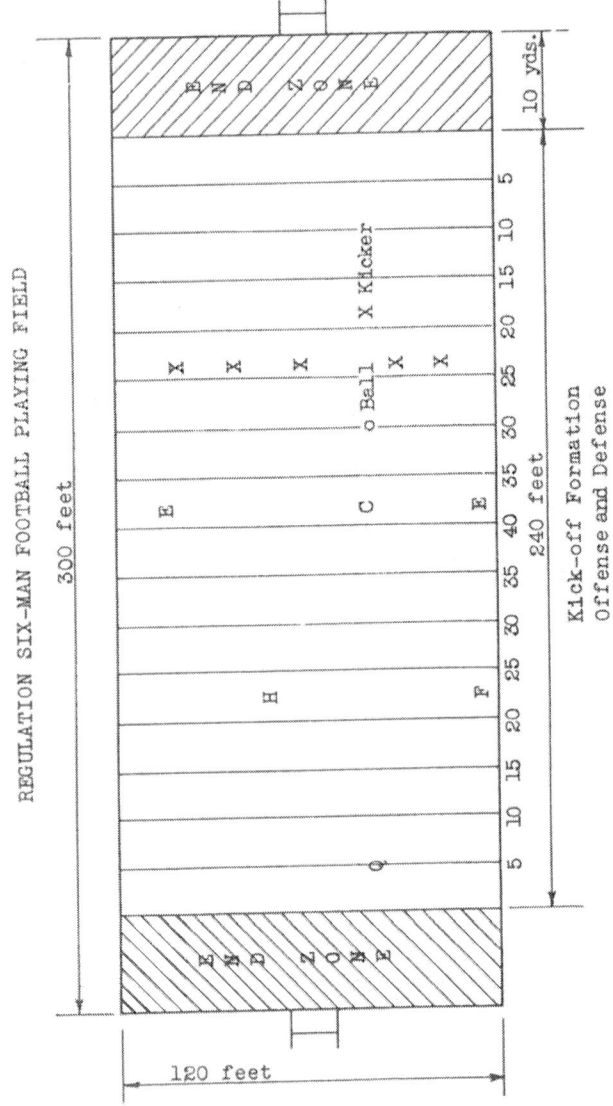

REGULATION SIX-MAN FOOTBALL PLAYING FIELD

300 feet

120 feet

240 feet

10 yds.

Kick-off Formation
Offense and Defense

TEAM STRATEGY IN SIX-MAN FOOTBALL

In Six-man football team strategy is divided
into two phases; offensive tactics and defensive
play. The coach must exert every effort to create a
harmonious balance between the two if his team is to
achieve most during the season's play. It would take
a top-heavy offense to counteract the weaknesses re-
sulting from a poor defense. The strongest defense
cannot make up for inability to score. In balancing
these two phases of the game the coach must study
his material and the strength and weaknesses of his
opponents. He must use his material in such a way
as to bring out every strong point it possesses and
reinforce in so far as is possible every existing
weakness. To do this successfully requires much
study and planning on the part of the coach.

Offensive strategy must consider:
a. The strength of its running attack
b. The effectiveness of its running attack
c. The success of its kicking offense
d. The type of defense used by the opponents
e. The weaknesses in the defense; both in
   formation and in personnel
f. Wind and weather conditions
g. The strategical situation; down, distance,
   score, time left to play; and, reserve
   strength
h. The psychological elements involved
Defensive strategy evolves around:
a. The formation used by the offense
b. The sequence of plays used
c. The strength and weakness of the offensive
   personnel
d. The favored style of attack used by the
   offense
e. The tactical situation
f. The score
g. The strength of offensive reserves
Against a team using a spread defensive

formation the offense should concentrate on its running attack and every effort should be made to draw
in the secondary defense for opening up favorable
situations for successful passing attack. Use those
plays that are successful until the defense stops
their effectiveness. Never vary the attack so long
as it is successful. Use the kicking and passing
attack against closely massed defensive formations
and when unexpected. Deception adds to the effectiveness of the offensive attack. Keep the ball as
long as possible against a team possessing a strong
offense and a weak defense. Take advantage of the
wind and of any abnormal weather conditions that
can be used in your favor. With the score close and
in your favor play a cautious game and hang on to
the ball. When behind in the last quarter hand the
defense everything you have and take chances. Your
only chance to win is to score much and as early as
possible. Since you are defeated as the score now
stands and an error will only add to the margin of
your defeat go after scores and take chances to get
them.

    Early in the game the quarterback or captain
should locate every evidence of weakness that the
opponents possess and should keep such evidence in
mind until an opportunity presents itself to use
your strength against this weakness. Often it is
wise to use such plays as are available that will
make small gains and then in the zone of intense resistance to use your strength against their weakness
for the scoring blow. It is extremely foolish to
aim plays against a weak man on the opposite team to
the point that his coach will remove him from the
game. Capitalize on weaknesses in defensive personnel when needed for scoring gains. Individual players can be of much value to the quarterback by re-
porting such weaknesses to him so that he can use
them to his teams advantage. The quarterback must
be alert for new situations and opportunities for
taking advantage of existing weaknesses.

The wind at one's back gives that team a decided advantage in passing and kicking and should be used accordingly. Rainy weather and a muddy field slows down the effectiveness of the passing, running, and kicking attack and requires a more conservative style of football than does ideal weather conditions. The presence of substitutes in the game often brings about weaknesses that can be used advantageously. Many coaches have a play aimed at the incoming substitute to test his ability and to demoralize his team's ability. The psychological factor here is important. It demoralizes a defense to have gains made over the incoming substitutes and causing a weakening of the co-operative efforts of the boys in many cases.

The calling of time-out at opportune times adds much to the effectiveness of the defense and the wise captain takes advantage of this period to discuss the game situation and to plan for coming events. He may re-assign men, bolster up the courage of lesser experienced men, encourage good performers, advise men on special assignments, and provide needed rest for his men in this interval. The coach should provide definite instructions for his captain regarding the taking advantage of the time-out. The coach should familiarize the boys with the situations where the time-out will be most valuable and should impress upon him the importance of taking it.

The captain should ask for substitutions when men are fatigued, injured and temporarily incapacitated. He is in better position to see evidences of impaired physical efficiency than is his coach in some cases and should exercise his prerogative. Against teams with limited reserves it is wise to rush the game and to permit no let-up on offense. A fast driving offense is very wearing on the physical resources and will weaken the defense if limited in reserve strength.

THE PLAY OF THE QUARTERBACK

The quarterback possesses the following qualifications if his position is to be best filled:

1. He must be alert and wide awake
2. He must know the personnel of his team and the strength and weaknesses of each man on the team.
3. He must be confident almost to the point of cockiness.
4. A good blocker.
5. Able to diagnose plays and sense game situations.
6. Have a thorough knowledge of fundamentals.
7. Possess a likeable personality and inspire confidence and respect from his team mates.
8. Be daring in his planning and imagination.
9. Willing to take chances and play the breaks of the game.
10. Be fearless in the face of adversity and when the going is tough.
11. Know when to pass and when not to pass.
12. Have confidence in his coach.
13. Possess a high resistance against injury. He can not shield injuries and guide a team successfully.
14. He must locate and play weaknesses in the defense.

On taking the field for a game the quarterback must:

a. Walk over the field to locate any wet spots, slippery areas, and unusual obstacles.
b. Note the direction and rate of the wind.
c. Survey the general lay-out of the field.
d. Decide upon his choice of options as provided in the rules.

e. See that every member of the starting
   line-up is thoroughly warmed-up before
   starting time.
f. Watch kickers and passers warm-up on opposing team.
g. Get final instructions from coach just
   prior to starting whistle.
h. Be thoroughly familiar with the ground
   rules and with the rules covering his
   duties.
i. Ask officials for any rules interpreta-
   tions which are not clear to him or which
   may be interpreted differently from how
   he is accustomed to have them interpreted.
j. See that all his men are ready for action
   when the whistle blows; all bandages and
   protective devices in place; all men with
   helmets on; etc.

The good quarterback will:
1. Ask the captain to take time out when the
   plays are failing to click.
2. Ask the captain to take time out when the
   opponents present a strange defensive or
   offensive formation.
3. Never allow time out to be called when
   his attack is going good. If a man is injured gather the team together and talk
   the game over to keep up courage while the
   injured man is being treated. Keep up the
   fighting spirit until play is resumed.
4. Allow no talking in the huddle. He must
   be the master.
5. Will talk over the various plays with the
   coach to determine which play will be
   best in a given situation.
6. Never talk about your team mates.
7. Never lose courage in face of defeat.
8. Study football; a quarterback who does
   not study football is a traitor to his
   coach and to his team.

9. Play low.
10. Hold the ball against a powerful offense.
11. Never quote the coach to other members of his team.
12. Remember what play works best.
13. Run a play at substitutes in the line to test their strength.
14. Let the other team carry the ball on a wet day and will watch for fumbles.
15. Gets his plays off fast when ahead or against a tired team.
16. Remember that he is in command on offense and that the captain is in command on defense.
17. Not run the star back too often.
18. Keep his team near midfield.
19. Not send his kicker into the line on the play before he must punt.
20. Never ask any favors.
21. Play safe conservative football when ahead.
22. Take chances in the last quarter if behind.

THE SCORE OF THE GAME AND THE TIME LEFT TO PLAY

At time "the score of the game and the time left to play" is the biggest factor is the selection of plays. I will list a number of various instances with suggestions.

1. When the score is tied or close, with plenty of time to play (normal conditions), this factor should be almost completely eliminated.

2. When you are ahead by a small margin and there is little time to play before the end of the game or half, unless you are in

good scoring territory, be exceptionally
cautious and take as much time as possible in getting off a play.

3. If you are behind by a small margin near
the end of the half, "cut loose" but don't
take desperate chances; but if near the
end of the game take any chance to score
if you are sure it is your last chance.

4. If you are more than one touchdown ahead,
irrespective of time left to play, be exceptionally cautious in dangerous territory but cut loose in scoring territory.

5. If you are more than one touchdown behind
cut loose in selection of big gainer
plays, but, if there is still plenty of
time to play don't stretch your kicking
rules too far; if there is but little
time to play take any chance.

6. Take no chances that may result in loss
of the ball when ahead near the half or
end of the game. PLAY SAFE.

The quarterback should watch the defense as
they line-up for the play and should note which men
show evidences of fatigue or injury and in planning
his attack should aim his power plays at those that
show evidences of fatigue or injury. The passing
attack should be aimed into those territories guarded by men handicapped by lack of speed, fatigue, or
injury. He should speed up his attack when confront-
ed by a tired, listless opposition. Nothing so de-
vitalizes a defense as to have an attack speeded up
at the onslaught of fatigue. The quarterback should
play for every advantage that can be had legally under the rules. Nothing succeeds like hard, driving,
fast clean football played by a team in fine physical

condition who can apply their knowledge of fundamentals and team strategy as a unit.

Gripers, trouble makers, and slackers should be reported to the coach before they damage the morale of the squad. Nothing impairs the efficiency of the offense like the presence of a loafer in a key position or a habitual griper who continually seeks trouble and encourages dissatisfaction and unrest among the team. Injured men should be replaced as a substitute in fine condition is more valuable than an injured regular.

THE DUTIES OF THE CAPTAIN

The captain has complete charge of the team on defense and is its official spokesman in dealing with the officials. He is responsible for the team's conduct on the field and for any requests to the officials for time-out, rules interpretation, choice of options on penalties, and for making choices as provided in the rules at the beginning of the first and third quarters of the game. He has complete charge of the team on the field. He should be thoroughly familiar with the rules covering the various penalties involving options in order to wisely choose those options most valuable to his team. He must be familiar with the style of play used by the opponents in order to best maneuver his defensive strength to stop their running, passing, and kicking attack.

The captain should take time out when the offensive team is overpowering his team or when they are gaining ground rapidly. He must take time out in case of an injury and should the injury show evidence of impairing the efficiency of the player should ask for a substitution. He should permit no time-outs when his team is going strong and making successful gains, as a time-out at this crucial time will permit the defense to organize their strength and may result in stopping the offensive attack.

Linemen should be encouraged in their efforts to stop the offense and commendation given to outstanding work on the part of team mates. Helpful criticism tactfully given will add to the ability of substitutes or men trying to stop a driving attack. The captain must not overdrive his men nor must he antagonize them by untactful remarks or profanity.

FIELD GENERALSHIP IN SIX-MAN FOOTBALL

The field general must have:
1. Courage
2. Initiative
3. Brains--knowledge of game and game conditions
4. Confidence of team
5. Good voice

The field general must consider:
1. Opponents
2. His plays
3. The players
4. Down and the distance to go
5. Score and the time left to play
6. Weather and wind
7. The position on the field

The field general must know:
1. When to kick
2. When to pass
3. When not to pass
4. When not to hit the line
5. When not to go wide
6. What to do on the goal line
7. When to attempt to catch passes on defense and when not to attempt to catch passes.

Strategy for downs:
On first down--try for touchdown
On second down--try for touchdown
On third down--try for first down
Your strategy for the fourth down depends
   upon the situation;
   a. Yardage to gain
   b. Position on field
   c. Time to half or end of game
   d. Own strengths and weaknesses

   The good field general must remember that
good generalship is just using good "Horse Sense."
   The good field general stresses the fact
that the best pass defense is to rush the passer. He
encourages the linemen to do this at all times.

BIBLIOGRAPHY

SIX-MAN FOOTBALL: Now is the time to organize for
Next fall. The Coach, 14:2, April, 1938
          A brief story of the rise and development
of Six-man football and the need for its organization in smaller schools. The author pleads for
the organization of leagues and conferences of
schools of similar size and competitive strength
in various sections of the country and discusses
some of the pitfalls of the game when poorly organized.

Stephen Epler: SIX-MAN OFFICIAL HANDBOOK, Price $.25
University Pub. Co., Lincoln, Neb., 1937
          A thorough explanation of the rules and
growth of the game. Shows offensive and defensive
formations together with coaching hints.

Leroy N. Mills: LICKING THE AMERICAN FOOTBALL,
G. P. Putman' Sons, New York. 1932. 156 pages
          A scientific treatment of the art and
place of kicking as a basic element in football
game success. Outlines a plan for the training of
outstanding kickers.

DaGrosa, John: FUNCTIONAL FOOTBALL, W. B. Saunders
Co., 1936. Philadelphia. 323 pages. $3.00
          One of the finest textbooks on football
fundamentals with special emphasis on the basic
principles of the game. The best book in the field
for inexperienced men who must attempt the coaching
of the game or who desire to acquaint themselves
with the finer points of the game.

Curtis, Esker: DEVELOPING PUNTERS IN HIGH SCHOOL,
Athletic Journal, December, 1932. Page 16 ff.

An outline for the teaching of beginners
in the essentials of punting and kicking. Good.

Crisler, H. O. and Wieman, E. E.: PRACTICAL FOOTBALL,
McGraw-Hill Book Co., New York. 1934. p. 242.
Price $3.00
          Intended as a guide in teaching and devel-
oping better technique and better coaching methods,
intended for persons having a knowledge of the
game. Special emphasis is given to blocking,
tackling, and the execution of fundamentals.

Epler, Stephen: FOOTBALL ARRANGEMENT FOR SIX PLAY-
ERS, Scholastic Coach, 5:16, September, 1935.
          An illustrated article dealing with the
arrangement of players for six-man football. Several offensive formations and plays from each formation are given. Each play is set-up against special defense best suited for its execution.

Stephens, M. A. and Phelps, W. M. THE CONTROL OF
FOOTBALL INJURIES, A. S. Barnes & Co. New York.
1933. p. 241. Price $3.00
          A treatise covering the techniques, pro-
cedures and practices having to do with the pre-
venting and care of football injuries. A valuable
addition to the coaches library.

Bierman, Bernie: WINNING FOOTBALL, McGraw-Hill Book
Company, New York. 1937. 276 pages. Price $2.50
          One of the finest discussions of the vari-
ous essentials of football available. The various
fundamentals are interestingly presented. His
chapter on tackling is a masterpiece.

Oakes, Bernard F.: FOOTBALL LINE PLAY, A. S. Barnes
& Co., New York, 1933. 258 pages
          A masterful presentation of the fundamen-
tals of modern line play interestingly and clearly
presented. Well illustrated and diagrammed. One
of the best textbooks on line play.

ARTICLES

Kelly, James D.: COACHING THE KICKER
Athletic Journal, 17:11-13, September, 1936
        An illustrated article on training the inex-
perienced kicker.

Boles, L. C.: PLAY OF THE BLOCKING BACK
Athletic Journal, 17:9-10, October, 1936
        A thorough but brief discussion of the duties
and techniques of the blocking back. Applicable to
six-man football.

Kizer, Noble: THE IMPORTANCE OF GOOD OFFENSIVE
                    BLOCKING
Athletic Journal, 17:10-13, November, 1936
        An excellently written and well illustrated
article on offensive blocking.

Larsen, A. W.: SIX-MAN FOOTBALL TOURNAMENTS
Athletic Journal, 18:12-13, November, 1937
        Suggest several plans for conducting tourna-
ments in six-man football for the purpose of deter-
mining championships. A fine reference for adminis-
trators planning to conduct such a contest.

Larson, A. W.: DEFENSE IN SIX-MAN FOOTBALL
Athletic Journal, 18:17-20, October, 1937
        A fine discussion of the essential elements
of a good team defense in six-man football. His the-
ory is sound and his illustrations very helpful.
Plots three diagrams of the most widely used defens-
es. This is one of the finest articles written on
the subject. Discusses the organization and carrying out of the game for the first season.

Epler, Stephen E.: RECENT TRENDS IN SIX-MAN FOOTBALL
Scholastic Coach, 7:17. September, 1937
        A brief summary of the development of six-man
football. Largely statistical in nature; no informa-
tion of special benefit to coaches.

Mills, Leroy N.: KICK IT WHERE YOU WANT IT
Scholastic Coach, 7:9-12, September, 1937
        One of the best articles on kicking to be
found in current literature. Very instructive and
well illustrated.

Cox, E. L.: ELMER HOLM'S DEFENSIVE LINE PLAY
Scholastic Coach, 7:7-10, October, 1937
        Contains much practical information on the
play of the line that would be applicable to six-man
football. The discussion of the center's play is
very good, and the play of the ends is most helpful.

Crisler, H. O. "Fritz": PROTECTING THE PASSER AND
                        KICKER
Scholastic Coach, 6:7-9, June, 1937
        A masterful presentation of the play of the
offense in protecting passers and kickers. Well illustrated and concisely written. Very helpful for
the inexperienced coach. Suitable for six-man football.

Made in the USA
Lexington, KY
31 October 2013